SYSTEMA COMBAT

RUSSIAN MARTIAL ART
25 COMBAT DRILLS

First Published in Great Britain 2016 by Mirador Publishing

First edition: 2016

A copy of this work is available through the British Library.

ISBN : 978-1-911473-24-4

Mirador Publishing
10 Greenbrook Terrace
Taunton
Somerset
TA1 1UT

SYSTEMA COMBAT

RUSSIAN MARTIAL ART
25 COMBAT DRILLS

MATT HILL

Warning

CONTENTS

ABOUT THE AUTHOR

Matt Hill is the owner and chief instructor at his Systema School in Wiltshire, UK. He started training in the Martial Arts in 1987 and by 1991 he was living as a full time student of Aikido giant Morihiro Saito in Iwama, Japan, where he lived for two years. Matt began his study of Systema in 2003. Matt is a qualified Systema Instructor under Vladimir Vasiliev, a 5th degree black belt in Aikido and an ex-Parachute Regiment Captain. He teaches full time at his school as well as leading workshops throughout the UK, Europe and the Middle East. He is committed to his personal training and sharing the gift of Systema with as many people as possible.

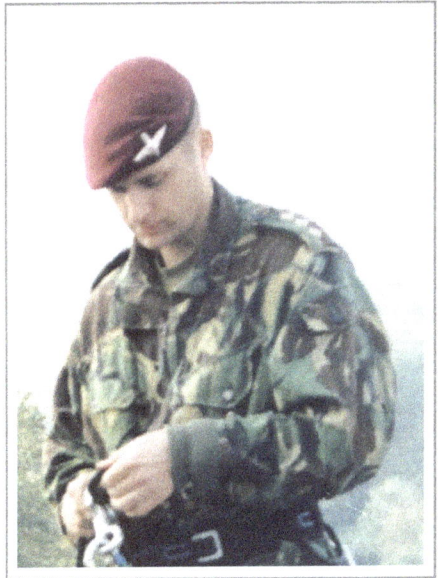

For more information, complimentary newsletters, details on seminars, training camps and instructional materials, visit

www.matthill.co.uk

ACKNOWLEDGEMENTS

They say that progression in anything is 1% inspiration and 99% perspiration. Actually, I have found that it is by the perspiration and support of many others, that real progress is achieved.

There are several people without whom this book would not have started. Mikhail Ryabko and Vladimir Vasiliev. I can't thank them enough for their guidance, example, genius and the willingness to share that with the world. Their experience and skill is hard won and they share it so openly and generously.

My special thanks also go to Haden Scott, Jason Rodwell, Karl Durrant, Gareth Leake and Kim Seviour for their help with the book. Specific thanks to Daniel Satari for his patience, skill and craftsmanship in helping to bring this book to life.

I could not pass this opportunity without thanking the Saito family in Iwama, Japan for kindling my passion for the Martial Arts and giving me so much at a very young age that has stayed with me. I would also like to thank my parents, for their continued love and support.

I also wish to thank my students, for allowing me to share with them my love and passion for Systema.

Lastly I would like to thank my wife Sarah, for her ongoing support and gentle encouragement to actually get this book finished to a deadline! Without her, it would still be sitting in a 'To Do' list.

FOREWORD BY VLADIMIR VASILIEV

DIRECTOR AND CHIEF INSTRUCTOR OF SYSTEMA HEADQUARTERS, TORONTO, CANADA

I would like to congratulate Matt on this publication.

It is always good to have an experienced professional become a Systema instructor.

In the time that I have known Matt, he has proved himself a strong and caring person, and a talented instructor.

Matt has been closely following the training methods taught by Mikhail Ryabko and myself. His understanding, willingness, and ability to share are very impressive.

Systema practice is beneficial for people of all ages and capabilities and Matt exemplifies this well in his teaching and in this publication.

Systema is now a widespread art, taught all over the world. I hope that with Matt's book more people will strengthen their health and martial art skills.

Vladimir Vasiliev, Toronto.
24th June 2016.

Systema Founder Mikhail Ryabko (left) and Systema HQ Director Vladimir Vasiliev in 2014 at the 'Legends of Systema' Seminar in Shropshire, in the United Kingdom. Mikhail and Vladimir are the two men largely responsible for the spread and popularity of Systema around the world.

INTRODUCTION

The roots of Systema go back ten centuries to the warriors and monasteries of Orthodox ancient Russia. Systema began to grow in popularity around the time of the collapse of the Soviet Union. Its popularity in recent times is largely due to two men: Mikhail Ryabko and Vladimir Vasiliev. Mikhail is a highly decorated Russian Army Colonel who received training from the age of five. From the age of fifteen he received combative training. He has been in numerous military campaigns and holds many medals and awards. He is the Master Teacher of Systema. Born in Russia Vladimir Vasiliev received intensive combative training and profound Systema training from Mikhail Ryabko. Vladimir is an exceptional student of Mikhail, and a decorated combat veteran. Since 1993 Vladimir has been based in Toronto, Canada and has been largely responsible for Systema's rapid growth outside Russia. Vladimir has trained and certified well over 600 instructors and schools in over 40 countries.

Systema or the System is a complete approach to combat skill. It is not a sport. It was developed for use by counter intelligence operatives and training incorporates more than just fighting skill. It deals with physical, psychological or emotional and spiritual aspects of your training. It is a holistic method of improving your health and your life. How can a martial art be both I hear you ask? Well, as Vladimir Vasiliev puts it, a good warrior is a healthy warrior, in body, mind and spirit for the whole of his life.

To really benefit from all that Systema has to offer, it should become a way of living, or being. You have to have faith in sacrificing old ways and habits of breathing, moving and thinking. Training is not solely limited to classes. It will naturally spill out into everyday life. Be hungry of spirit and willing to discover new skills, feelings and horizons within yourself. It's a journey and not a destination and each step on the journey is filled with unexpected benefits. Many people describe Systema as a cleaning system. A way to rid your mind, body and spirit of the tension, fears and anxieties that daily living puts in. Tension restricts your movement, thought, action, sense of ease and peace and when that tension becomes chronic, your very life expectancy also becomes limited.

I feel very much like a beginner on this journey. Every day I enquire deeper into myself through Systema. In the pages of this book I have outlined some of the combat enhancing drills that I have learned from my teachers. I hope that it will support beginners who are just starting their Systema journey and also beginners like myself, who have been studying for much longer. It is my hope that readers will use these drills to enquire deeper of themselves and as a guide to share Systema with others.

It is important to note that this book is not meant to replace a teacher. Even if you do not have a teacher locally enough to train regularly, you should try to get to seminars with a recognized Systema Instructor. Development in Systema requires guidance and support from someone with a deep knowledge of its methods and principles. The art of finding a good teacher is easy. Look at their students.

Lastly I would say this. Training in Systema is fun. It brings deep joy and a sense of peace. Enquire deeply, train with every fibre of your being, try to live it, in every movement and breath and your progress and health will surely improve. As Vladimir Vasiliev says, "The beauty of Systema is that as your combat skill improves, so does your health."

I have created a video for each of the practises that is free for owners of the book. You can view the videos by using this link: http://www.matthill.co.uk/combat-videos

"A straight body removes fear and agression from you."
– Vladimir Vasiliev

TRAINING TOOLS

A compass and map for your journey

Begin with pushes not strikes. In many of the drills you push or strike. As your skill develops, this will naturally progress to faster and stronger pushes and/or strikes over time. Try to spend a lot of time with just pushes. Your reward for this patience is a strong, deep strike that is readily deployable when needed.

You are both working, all of the time. With all drills in Systema, whether you are feeding attacks or receiving attacks you are both working, so make sure that no part of the work is done mindlessly. In many ways you learn Systema by having it done to you. **The skill is transmitted body to body**. So when you feed attacks to your partner, be completely aware and conscious and do it with every fibre of your being.

Adjust the volume. First work at a slow walk to build the skill, then fast walk, then run. If you find yourself continually making mistakes slow it down again, find and fix the problem and then gradually speed up again.

Variety is the spice of life -and Systema: Don't always stand straight on. Vary it. Stand side on, with your back to the partner, oblique. Work all the angles. Remember that Systema is not training for a ring or mat where you are ready, it is for outside where you could be in any position at any time and in any state of readiness.

Play, experiment and explore. Systema does not teach through a set series of kata or techniques. It is important to note that the pictures shown are intended as a guide only and show just one way of doing things. There are in fact an infinite number of ways to respond in almost every case. Play with the principles, experiment and explore infinite variety. Try it with your eyes closed, in a corner, in a tight space, with hands tied etc. Have fun but stay safe. My deep desire is that through the logical progressions in these drills, you will begin freely creating your own drills, to the extent where you are training in Systema in every moment. By all means use my progressions as a guide, but you then have to just move randomly and naturally. Try not to form patterns in your movements.

It all boils down to movement. Really Systema is the study of movement. We study body movement, relaxation, breathing and footwork so as not to rely on strength or speed. There will always be a time when you lose those. In Systema, we train to survive and prevail through superior movement.

Work from contact. An inevitability of combat is that you will get hit. In Systema we do a lot of work from contact, for practical and psychological purposes. There will be times when you haven't had chance to block, redirect or move. Contact drills teach the body and psyche to deal with hits and to look after themselves. You learn body intelligence.

Finally, it begins and ends with the breath. Systema begins and ends here. Try to notice every time you hold your breath. Every time you hold your breath and move, tension and fear will come into your body. To be truly free in your movements, you have to be free in your breath. Always look to make your breath the engine or driver of your movement, not a 'by product' of it.

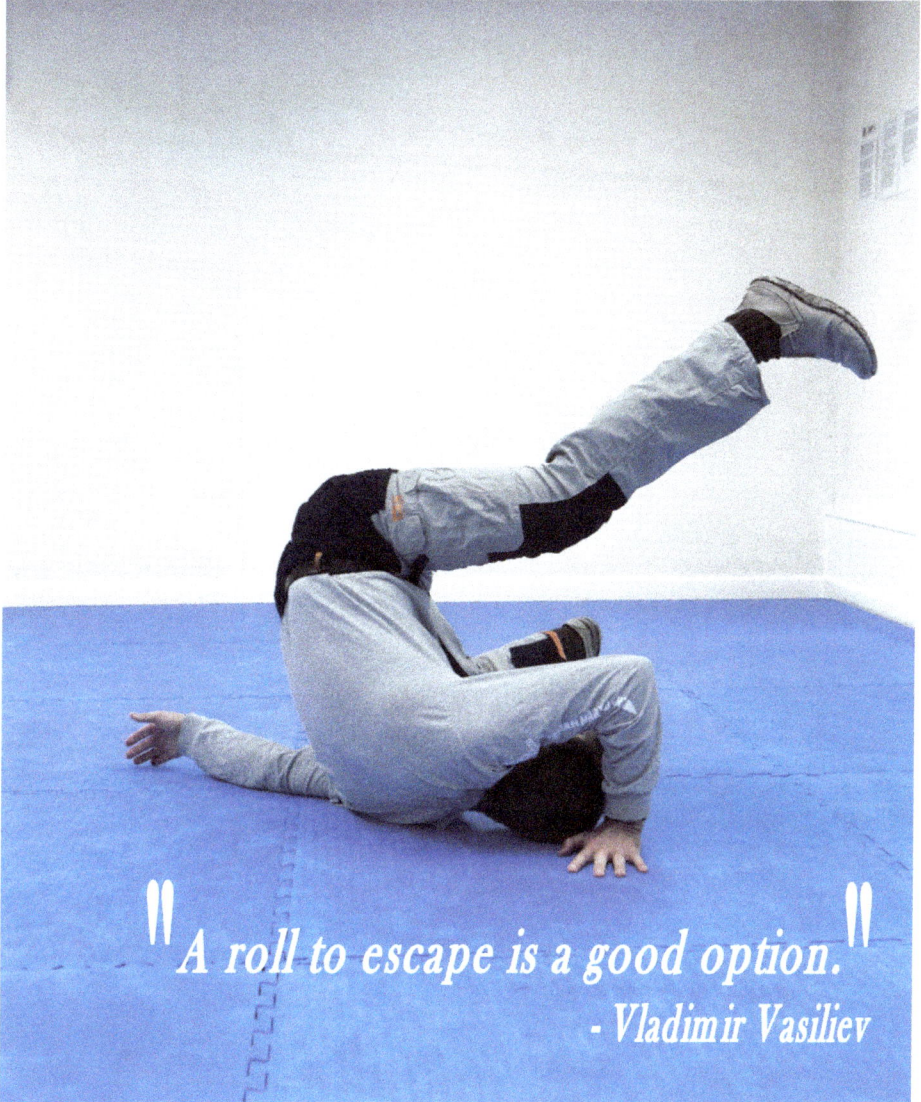

"A roll to escape is a good option."

- Vladimir Vasiliev

DRILL 1

STATIC PUSH DRILLS

The softer you get the stronger you get

Even for people that have no martial arts experience, this is a great drill to let first session beginners know they are doing a martial art. As with all drills in Systema, whether you are feeding attacks or receiving them, you are both working. The aim is to receive the pushes in a way that doesn't resist them.

The receiver stands on the spot as the feeder moves around the body, placing their hands and pushing. As your partner pushes you exhale and then go with the direction of the push, not letting pressure build up in your body. For the purpose of this drill, try not to step as you get pushed. Begin very slowly with gentle pushes and as your skill develops progress to faster and stronger pushes over time. The feeder should also exhale with every push to 'drill' in this aspect. This drill teaches the body to take care of itself, to yield to force whilst staying soft. Try to retain a good posture, but not at the price of over tensing the body. If you need to sacrifice posture for a moment do so, then rebuild your structure again immediately.

Push all parts of the body, top, bottom, sides, front and back. It is important that you get comfortable with all angles and contact in all areas of the body.

Progression: After about ten minutes change roles. Then try the exercise as a game. Both of you push and yield, the aim being to make the other person take a step.

To view the free video of this practise please use the link below:

http://www.matthill.co.uk/combat-videos

DRILL 2

FIST WALK
Acclimatising you to pressure

In the Fist Walk drill both people are again working. In this drill you are learning where and how to strike. In terms of where to strike, the 'walker' is learning to make a comfortable placement of their fist on the partner. A comfortable spot is one that is a stable placement that you don't slide off.

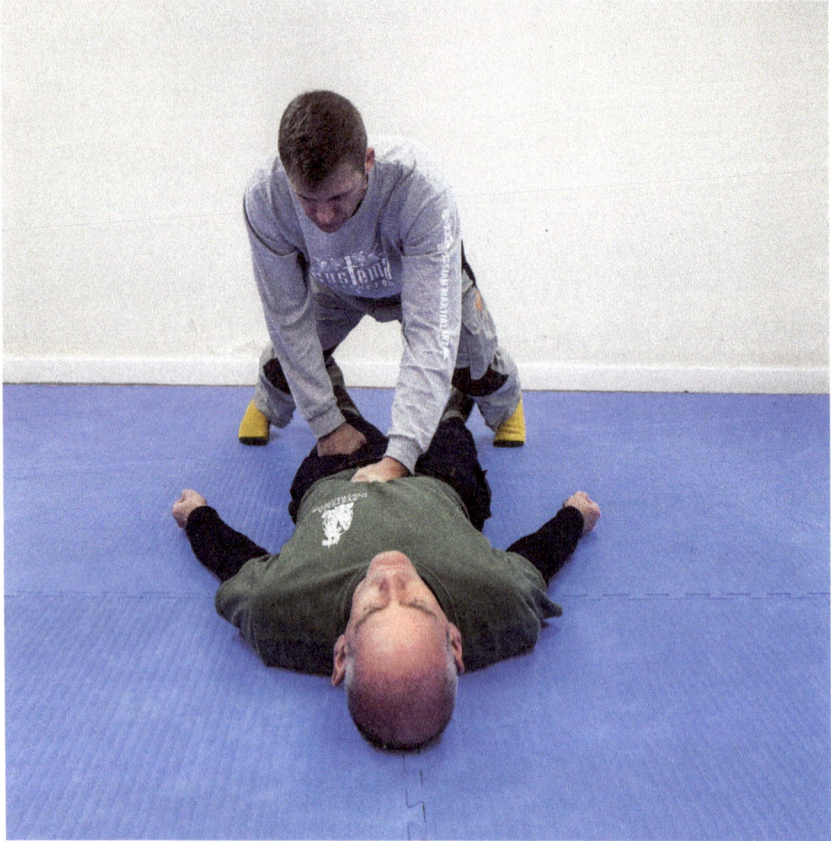

Look for muscles not bones. This way when you come to strike, the hand won't get injured. Experiment on the whole body, front and back. The 'walker' is looking for good alignment in the arm and wrist, so that when their weight travels through the fist it doesn't collapse. The body and especially shoulders should be relaxed. Your breath shouldn't be held. The receiver practices relaxed breathing and trying not to tense up, as the 'walker' places the weight of their body onto the muscles.

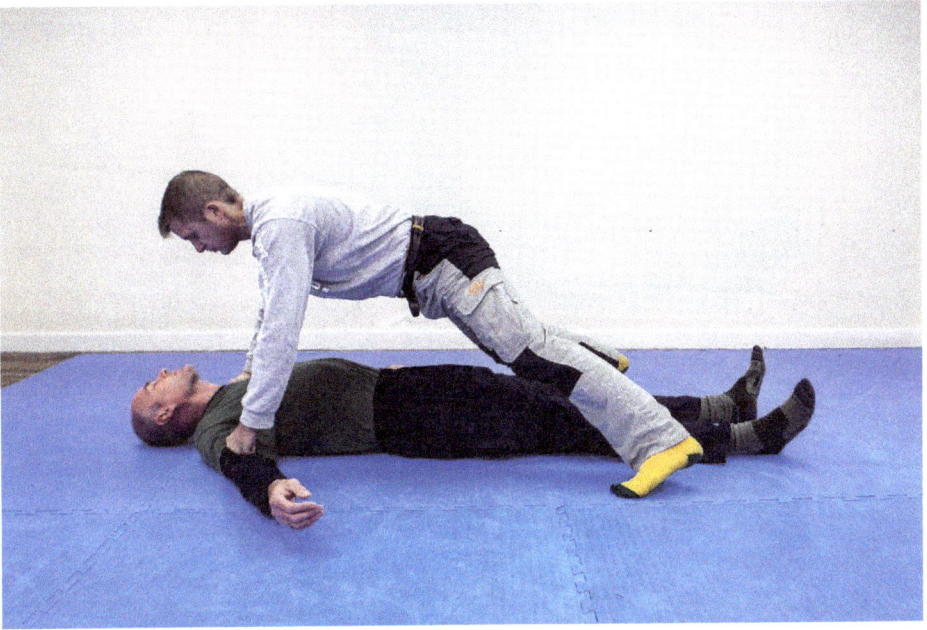

This exercise is hard for both feeder and receiver. You may need to adopt 'burst breathing' (Drill one in Systema Health). This is a rapid cycle of nasal inhale followed by an exhale through the mouth.

Progression. *Try to test the weight of the body through one wrist, as shown below. If you can do this, try to do push ups with two hands and then one hand.*

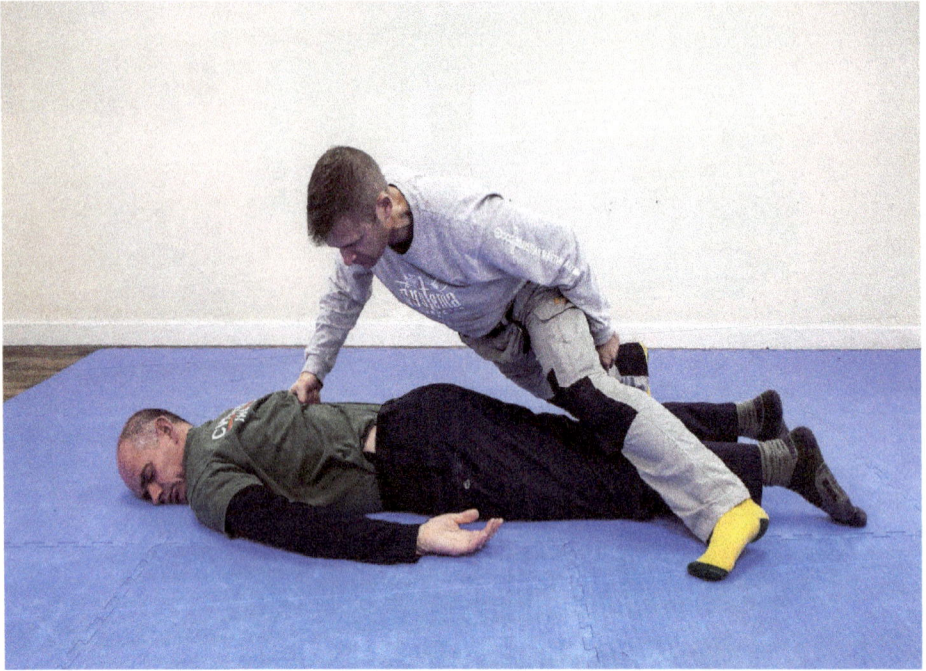

To view the free video of this practise please use the link below:

http://www.matthill.co.uk/combat-videos

DRILL 3

WASHING PUSH STRIKES

Acclimatising to strike work

This is a progression of Drill 1 and it enables both the feeder and the receiver to acclimatize themselves to push strikes. The receiver stands on the spot as the feeder moves around the body, placing their fist and pushing. As per drill 1, the aim is to teach the body to protect itself, as you yield to force whilst staying soft and well structured in a good posture, able to work. All areas of the body should be pushed including front, back, top and bottom. Especially do not neglect the face, as this for many is a very emotional area. When you find a strong emotion surface during this drill, such as fear or aggression, notice it and try to dissolve the emotion with correct breathing, 'burst breathing' (See Drill 1 Systema Health) if need be.

Important Note. *Many people find striking psychologically harder than being struck. By doing the drill as a push, you begin to acclimatize yourself gently. It is very important to exhale when both placing the fist and when receiving it.*

To view the free video of this practise please use the link below:

http://www.matthill.co.uk/combat-videos

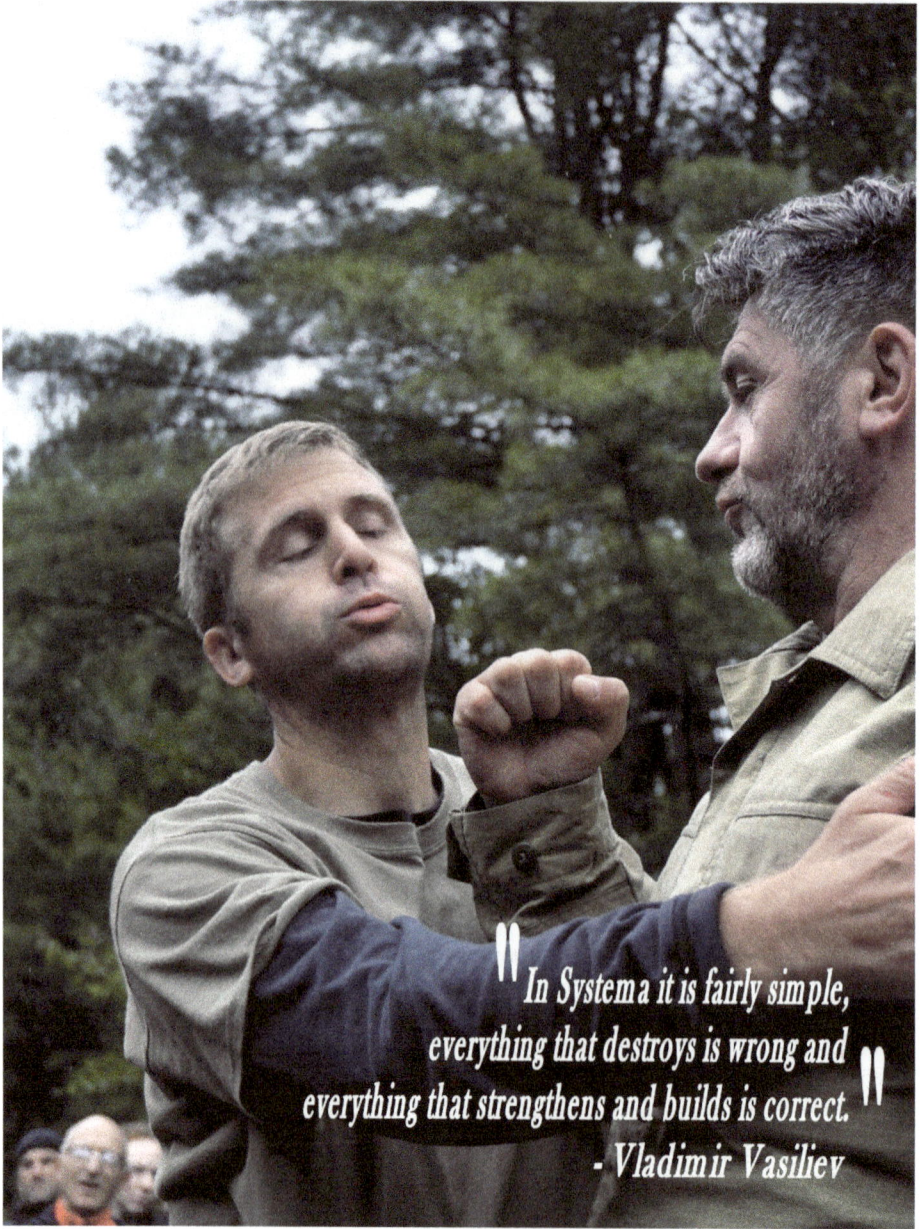

In Systema it is fairly simple, everything that destroys is wrong and everything that strengthens and builds is correct.
- Vladimir Vasiliev

DRILL 4

WASHING IMPACT STRIKES

This is a progression of Drill 3. This static drill takes the acclimatization to the next level: Impact. You now strike rather than push. Start slow and soft, gradually building up. It is important to watch the person's response as you strike. The receiver stands on the spot as the feeder moves around the body delivering strikes. Both partners should remain casual and relaxed. The feeling of the strike is akin to slapping a friend on the shoulder, relaxed, heavy and friendly. Aim to 'drop' the fist onto your partner rather than push from the shoulder and back. Notice the receiver's breathing and body language. If they start to hold their breath or become tense or agitated, you should ease off on the intensity.

Important note: *Vladimir Vasiliev says that in Systema it is simple: 'Everything that destroys is wrong and everything that strengthens and builds is correct.'* To this end make sure that during this drill, you are not putting more fear into your partner. You should be helping them to remove fear.

To view the free video of this practise please use the link below:

http://www.matthill.co.uk/combat-videos

DRILL 5

LONG WORK WITH STRIKES

When you make mistakes in training, make BIG ones

This drill makes drills 1, 3 and 4 dynamic. It gives you the space to cognitively learn. So if you make mistakes you make BIG ones. This way you see it, your instructor sees it and together you can correct it faster, improving your skill.

Both partners move their feet during this drill. Try to maintain the key principles of walking, as per health drills 3 and 16 in the Systema Health book. The feeder feeds in strikes and the receiver reaches out to meet the strike, receives and avoids it. It is important not to redirect the strike. The hand that receives should be like an insect's antenna, not so strong that you push or block your partner. You should use the contact with your arms to move your body out of the way, rather than using your hand to move their attack out of the way.

Practise this drill until it becomes smooth, with both hands from any position and even with multiple opponents.

As your skill improves progress to counter strikes. Try to avoid and deliver a counter strike at the same time. You should attempt to do this in one movement or beat, not two. It helps to work to a beat in your head, 1, 1, 1, 1, 1, etc. So on every beat, you should avoid and counter in the same instant. This is much harder to defend against.

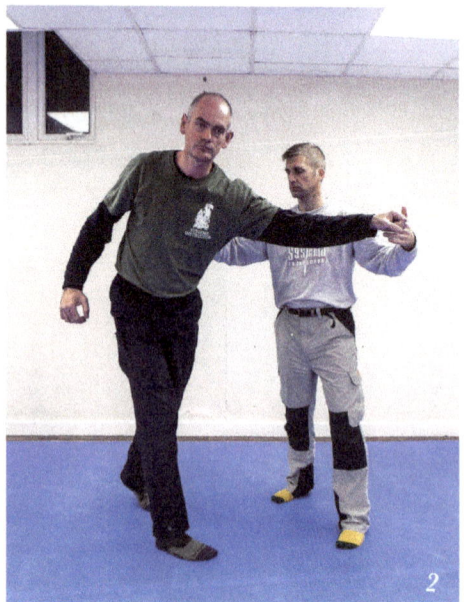

To view the free video of this practise please use the link below:
http://www.matthill.co.uk/combat-videos

DRILL 6

STAMP DRILL

Go with the flow

This drill replicates a common self-defence situation where you are on the floor and someone comes in to stamp on you.

You work from contact i.e. you have not had chance to block, redirect or move. The drill teaches the body to look after itself. You learn body intelligence.

The receiver goes to ground. The feeder comes to stamp. The key for the receiver is to use his breathing to stay calm. Don't resist the stamp.

Feel the direction of the foot, maintain contact with it and move your body in that direction. Gather/collect yourself around that point and keep rolling.

Notice the point where the energy dissipates from the attack. At this point the feeder ceases to be the positive force and the receiver takes the lead becoming the positive one. The feeder then loses balance and falls safely.

Progression: Change the position that you take on the floor each time. Front, back, side, crouch on knees etc. Then progress to rolling smoothly to a standing position and escaping or following up with a kick, stamp or strike of your own as shown in the pictures below and overleaf.

Tip: You don't make them change what they do. Let them stamp as they want to do it. They should think that they have succeeded until they start to fall over.

To view the free video of this practise please use the link below:

http://www.matthill.co.uk/combat-videos

DRILL

7

KICK DRILL

It's all in the timing, blend with the kick

For this drill the feeder attacks with kicks. The drill can be done in two stages. In the first stage the receiver avoids the kick totally, or redirects the kick with their body and places their foot down next to the feeders foot as it lands (close up image 3). Practise this with all kinds and directions of kicks, until the movement and timing are smooth. The next stage is to then sweep the feeder's foot out with yours, just as it is about to land. The feeder needs to be prepared to fall safely and remember to exhale while doing so.

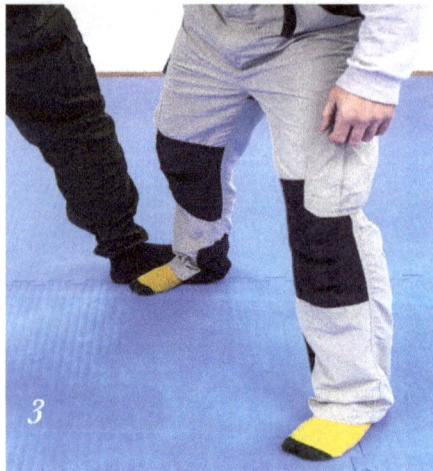

For the feeder, the feeling is like slipping on a banana skin.

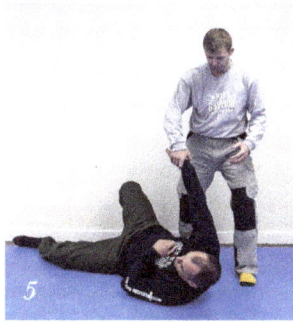

The picture above (7) shows a position than can result from sweeping the leg from the inside, rather than the outside as in the previous example.

To view the free video of this practise please use the link below:

http://www.matthill.co.uk/combat-videos

DRILL 8

DRONE ATTACK

Teaching distance & awareness

You can do this drill with one partner or several as shown in the pictures. Here the feeder(s) pick a line and walk that line through the receiver. It is important that the feeders keep the original line of attack and not follow the receiver as they move off line. The aim for the receiver is to avoid being hit. The key is to move out of the way: *just in time and just enough*. You can begin this as a static drill and then progress to continual movement with multiple partners.

First work at a slow walk to build the skill, then fast walk, then run. If you find yourself continually making mistakes slow it down again, fix the problem and then gradually speed back up.

Progressions: Next try with the feeders having their fist extended from the body to acclimatise to the different distance and then finally try with normal strikes.

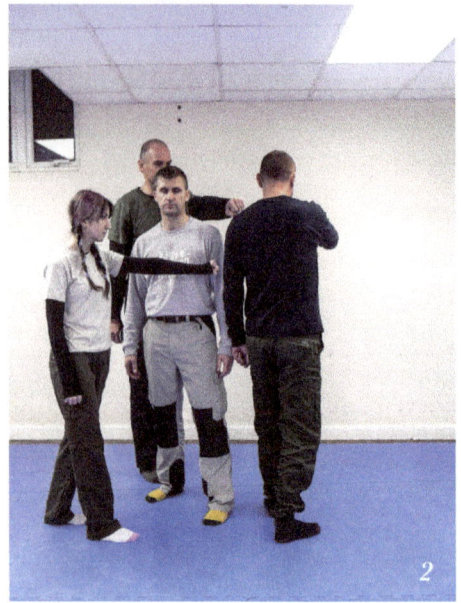

Tip: don't always stand straight on. Stand side on, with your back to the partner, oblique etc. Work all the angles. Remember that Systema is not training for a ring or mat where you are ready; it is for outside, where you could be in any position at any time and any state of readiness.

To view the free video of this practise please use the link below:

http://www.matthill.co.uk/combat-videos

DRILL 9

WEAPON FAMILIARITY

If you can't smoothly draw and use it when you need it, you may as well be unarmed.

This drill is designed to acclimatise you to being comfortable working with weapons. Here we use a knife and a stick. You could do the same with a gun, chain or other types of weapon. It is important to work with different size and shape weapons. Begin with the act of drawing and concealing the weapon. First just walk and practise drawing and concealing the weapon, without extra movement in the shoulders. Then try going to ground and standing again as in the images below.

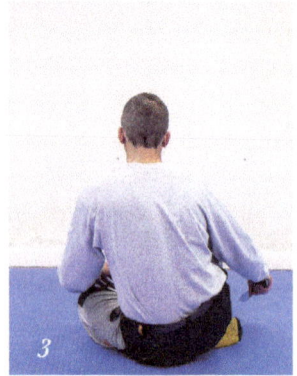

Understand positions on the body where it is comfortable and easy to draw from. Then explore other places such as cross body movements, in your sock, up your sleeve etc. Through this practise you develop an understanding of good and bad places to conceal weapons and the movement's people make to draw them.

Important note: *This drill is not designed to make you a stealthy attacker. As you practise you begin to understand how someone with the intent to hurt you may think and work, where they may conceal weapons, what movements may give this away. By learning how to attack you learn how to protect yourself and others. You also become a better training partner by providing good, realistic attacks.*

The pictures below show work with a long stick. Begin by walking and moving it around the body, then progress to going to ground and back up again.

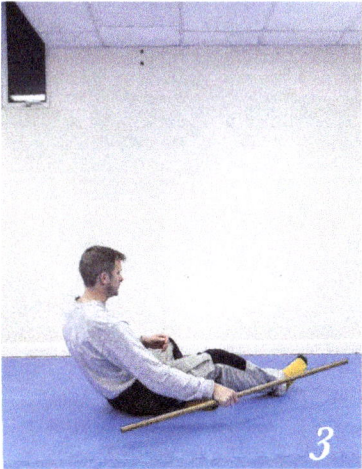

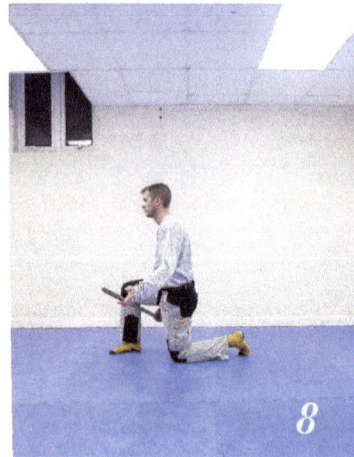

Progression: Do the drill slow, fast, forward and backwards, walking and running. Also do it in a crowd so that you can observe others. Then try it doing more complex movements such as getting up and down and rolling etc. Feel free to be creative here, such as trying it when getting in and out of a car, while putting your jacket on etc.

Practise so you are completely comfortable and familiar with the weapon in any position or movement so that there is no barrier to you using it effectively. Then you will understand how others may use it against you.

To view the free video of this practise please use the link below:

http://www.matthill.co.uk/combat-videos

DRILL

10

HEADLOCK

Working with a very common attack

The pictures show three ways to manage the situation. First, by bringing the shoulder to the ear. It is important to close the gap between the jaw and the shoulder, by bringing the shoulder to ear so that the attacker's arm cannot get hold.

Option 1: *Raising the shoulder*

2

3

Option 2: Ducking the head

In the second instance, you duck the head forward so that the attack slips over the top.

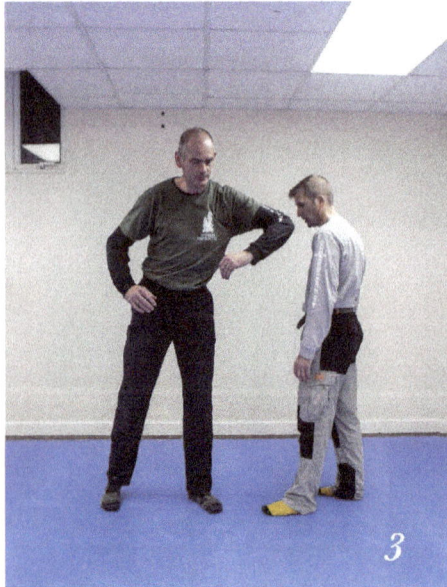

Progression: Once you are comfortable with two methods of defence, try to add in offensive work such as strikes or structure breaks.

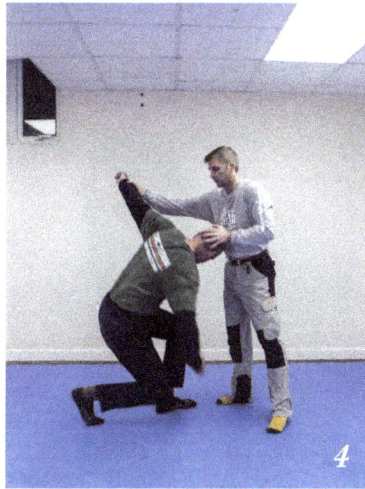

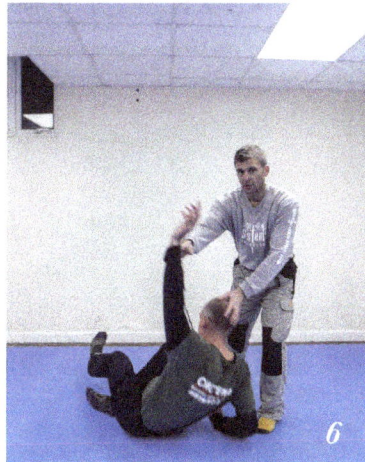

Option 3: Swimming

In the third instance, you move out of the attack with a 'swimming' like movement. If there are other attackers, you can use this to go straight into an offensive movement and follow up with a push or strike as in the pictures.

There are lots of options, so please explore the drill from as many different angles and situations as possible.

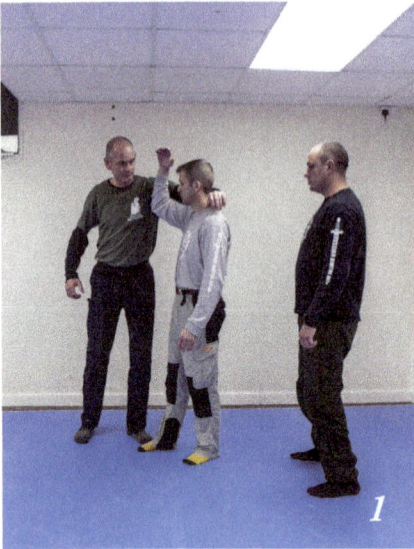

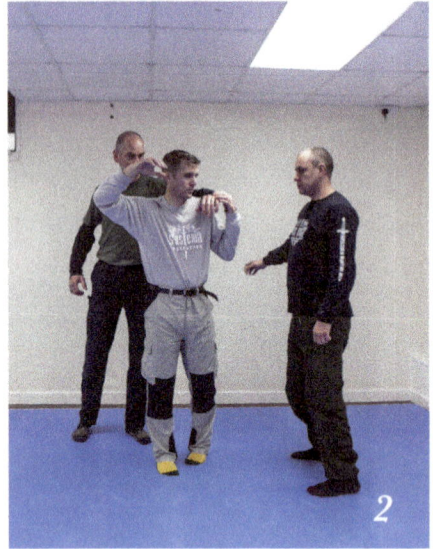

To view the free video of this practise please use the link below:

http://www.matthill.co.uk/combat-videos

"Tension in your body,
is a manifestation of
fear at some level."
- Mikhail Ryabko

DRILL

11

STRUCTURE SEVEN LEVELS
Breaking structure for take downs

This is a basic drill that teaches how to break a person's structure to take them down. There are 7 basic places where structure can be taken: the head, shoulders, elbows, wrists, hips, knees and ankles. As always there are an infinite number of angles that can be used, so please experiment from all directions and angles.

Head

Shoulders

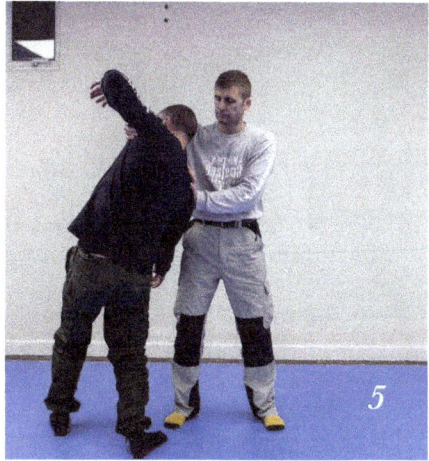

Elbows

Hips

Knees

Ankles

The person being taken down should exhale as they fall and learn to fall softly and safely.

Progression: Try to combine different body parts such as head and wrist, or hip and elbow. When you can work comfortably with structure make the drill dynamic, so try the drone attack (drill 8) and take the feeder down on the move. Then try it against attacks such as grabs, kicks, strikes and weapons.

To view the free video of this practise please use the link below:

http://www.matthill.co.uk/combat-videos

DRILL 12

GROUND WRESTLING

Move and explore like tiger cubs

This drill will soften the body and prepare you psychologically for ground movement. Here both partners just wrestle freely on the ground. Use the drill to explore movement and good and bad positions. Key points to work on are your breathing (inhale through the nose and exhale through the mouth) and moving continuously and efficiently with as little effort as possible. Don't hold your breath or you will get tired very quickly.

It is important not to get fixated on winning or losing. Just move and explore like tiger cubs playing. If you attain a good position just give it up and move. Equally, if you are in a bad position manage your breathing and work out how to move and escape.

To view the free video of this practise please use the link below:
http://www.matthill.co.uk/combat-videos

"Progress comes in hills and plateaus. Understand this and your approach to training becomes much more relaxed."

-   Matt Hill

DRILL 13

DYNAMIC PUSH DRILLS
As light as a feather or as heavy as lead

This drill is used to practise making the body heavy or light, depending on the requirement.

Light Movement: As your partner pushes, practise moving with or just ahead of their push, so that you feel very light to them. You are light on your feet, much like a matador in a bullfight. Make sure that you move just in time, not too early or too late. You should be a hairs breadth ahead of your partner's movement.

Heavy Movement: As your partner pushes, you move only as far as they push. No more and no less. You don't resist, but neither do you travel more than the push propels you. To do this you need to relax and make your body heavy. To your partner it should feel like pushing a sandbag up hill.

As you get better at this drill, the feeling is like slowing down time as you move, giving you more time to think about what you are going to do.

To view the free video of this practise please use the link below:
http://www.matthill.co.uk/combat-videos

"I'm not flexible, I'm just free."

- Vladimir Vasiliev

DRILL

14

PIGGY IN THE MIDDLE

Sitting, kneeling, standing

In this drill you begin sitting with a partner either side of you. Their job is to push you over. Your job is to stay in a sitting position. You need to ride their pushes with good movement and breathing. The feeling is like 'swimming' through their pushes. This is an excellent drill to practise the feeling of not giving your partner(s) tension or support to push you over.

Progression: In the second instance, you also disrupt them to practise being able to simultaneously ride their pushes and disrupt and push them back, without having to use tension to generate the push; to find power without support. In the third progression you all strike and push. Ride the pushes and strikes and strike in return.

1. SWIM

2. DISRUPT

3. STRIKE

You can then try the same drill and progressions in the kneeling and standing positions.

1. SWIM

2. DISRUPT

3. STRIKE

Safety note: When doing the kneeling progression, learn to fall backwards off the knees safely. To do this you sit to the side, onto your backside and then roll onto your back. It is important to practise this as a solo drill, before you practise it under pressure in the partner drill.

1. SWIM

2. DISRUPT

3. STRIKE

To view the free video of this practise please use the link below:

http://www.matthill.co.uk/combat-videos

DRILL
15

KNIFE LIFE SAVER

Practising survival

In the case of a real attack, it is possible that the first you know that you are under attack is when you are hit (opposite picture). Your response to this can be the difference between success and failure: surviving, or not. This drill is designed to teach the body to look after itself, when you are not aware of the attack.

For an untrained person, their first response is to tense up and hold their breath. In this drill your partner pushes you with the knife from different angles all around the body. Your job is to breathe and move in the direction of the knife when it contacts you. Keep the body soft. It is a survival drill.

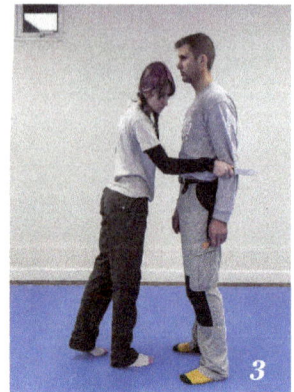

Progression: Practise with eyes open and then once comfortable, practise with your eyes closed. This will help to make your response more spontaneous.

To view the free video of this practise please use the link below:

http://www.matthill.co.uk/combat-videos

DRILL

16

KNIFE WASH

Developing sensitivity to the knife

In this drill you develop sensitivity and hand to blade orientation. The feeder stabs towards the body. The receiver makes a motion as though they are 'washing their body' i.e. the palm of the hand is in contact with the body between the knife and the body. The knife gets 'washed' past, similar to the long work drill (drill 5). The hand informs the body as to how to move just like an insect's antennae.

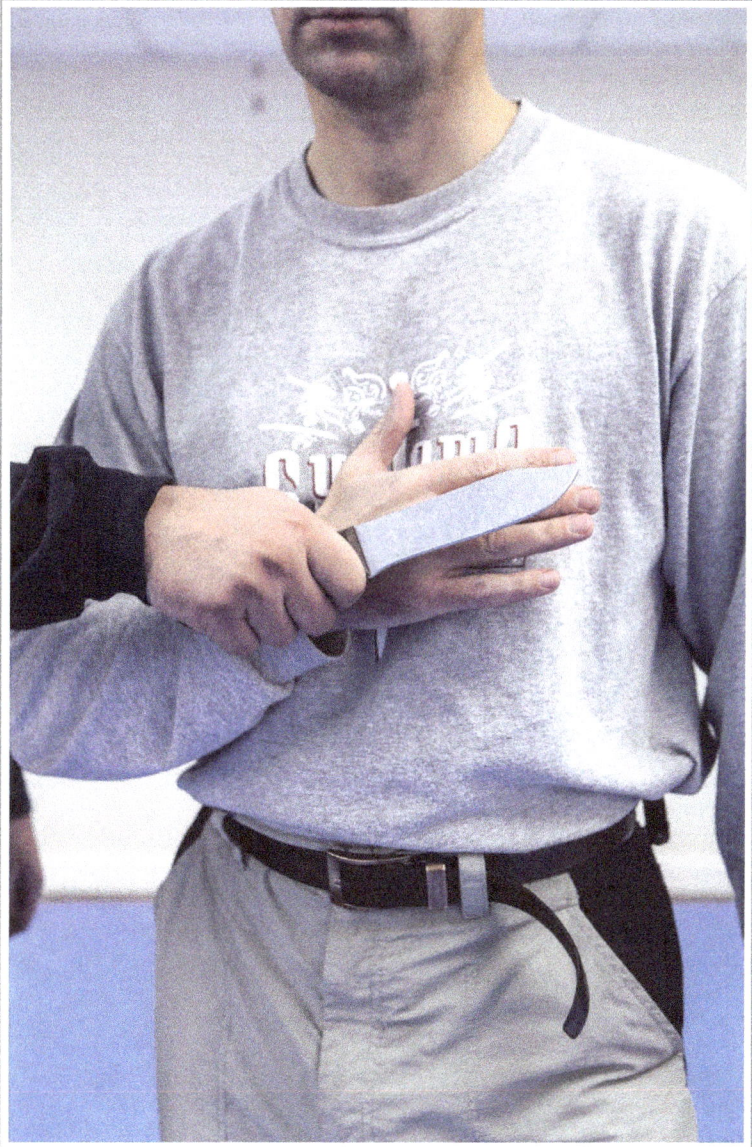

Remember not to push the knife out of the way, instead move your body. The feeder should feed attacks in from all angles and types of knife hold. The more variety the better. Exhale each time that you defend or attack.

Progressions: Once you are comfortable with the action of 'washing', try to smoothly move into structure breaking, escape, disarm, drawing your own weapon or other options as appropriate.

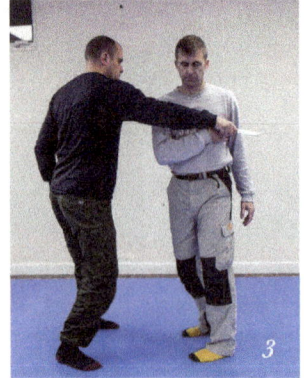

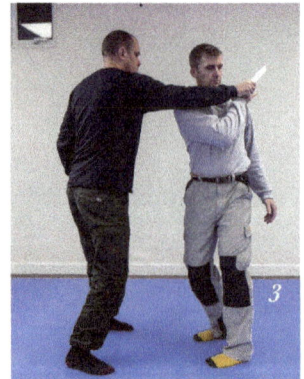

To view the free video of this practise please use the link below:
http://www.matthill.co.uk/combat-videos

DRILL

17

KNIFE HOLD

Learning to disarm & retain

This drill teaches you two skills. Knife retention and the skill of removing the knife from the attacker's grasp. One partner holds the knife loosely as per the picture. The other then grasps the knife and tries to remove it from the hand. The job of the first partner is to retain the knife.

The skill is to use good footwork and body movement to retain the knife and not just hand strength or speed. There will always be a time when these are not enough.

In Systema we seek to prevail through superior movement skill. Look for effective angles and levers.

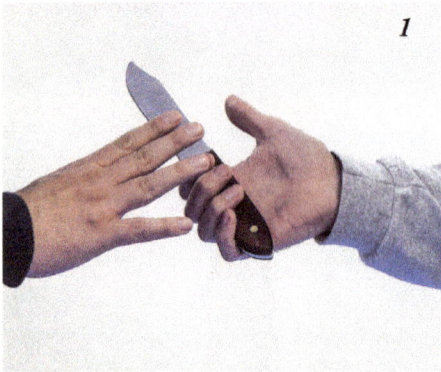

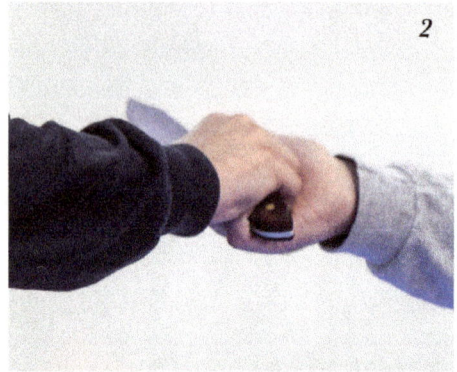

It is important to hold the knife in different ways and to try to remove the knife in different ways, in order to work as many variations as possible.

Progression: Try the drill from different positions e.g. with one on the ground and one standing; both on the ground; one or both sitting in a chair etc.

Alternate Grasp

To view the free video of this practise please use the link below:

http://www.matthill.co.uk/combat-videos

DRILL 18

BODY REMOVALS
Combining drills 17 and 15

As the knife makes contact, the receiver pins the knife to the body. It is important that as the knife is trapped, you strive to maintain the flat of the blade against the body. The receiver then moves the body to apply a lever to the wrist and fingers forcing the attacker to release their hold on the knife.

Try to remove the knife with the same hand that pinned it to the body in order to keep the remaining hand free to do other work.

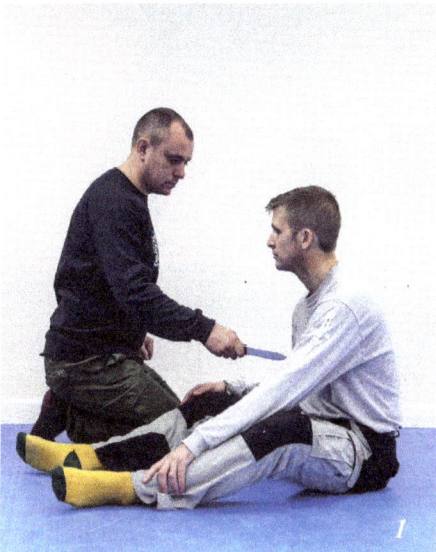

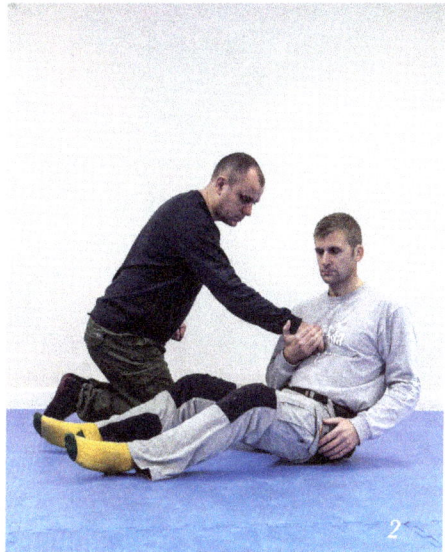

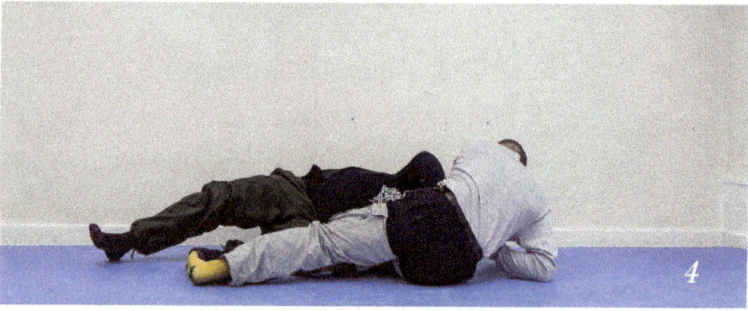

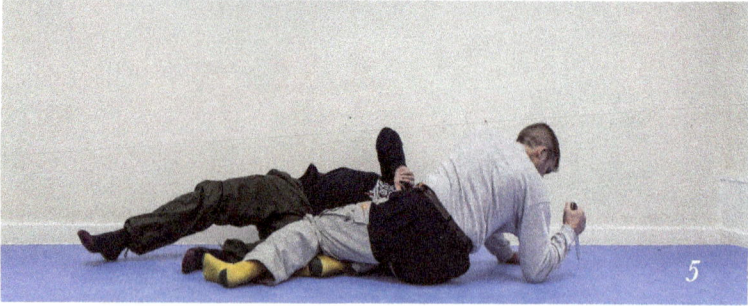

This drill should be practised in standing, sitting and lying positions.

2

3

To view the free video of this practise please use the link below:

http://www.matthill.co.uk/combat-videos

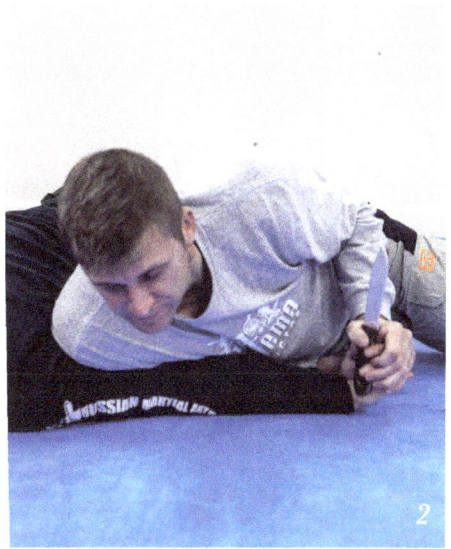

Important: Your breathing will become important in order to manage your energy levels and anxiety or excitement. Work to make your breathing like a pump that fuels your movement. Not a ragged 'by-product' of your movement.

To view the free video of this practise please use the link below:

http://www.matthill.co.uk/combat-videos

DRILL 20

KNIFE STRUCTURE BREAK

From instinct to knowledge

In this drill we work from a common response to being attacked with a knife. The feeder attacks and the receiver grasps the knife hand. Try to keep your arm loose and your grip strong. As the feeder continues to the stab, the receiver's relaxed arm informs them of the direction of the strike and allows them to move the body out of the way. Pressure is then applied to a weak area of the feeder's body to break the structure and take the attacker to ground. Ensure that you take the knife from the attacker utilising the 'knife hold' drill (17).

This is a good drill to practise going from instinctive tension (in the initial grab) to applying the knowledge of relaxation to let the knife pass and disarm the attacker.

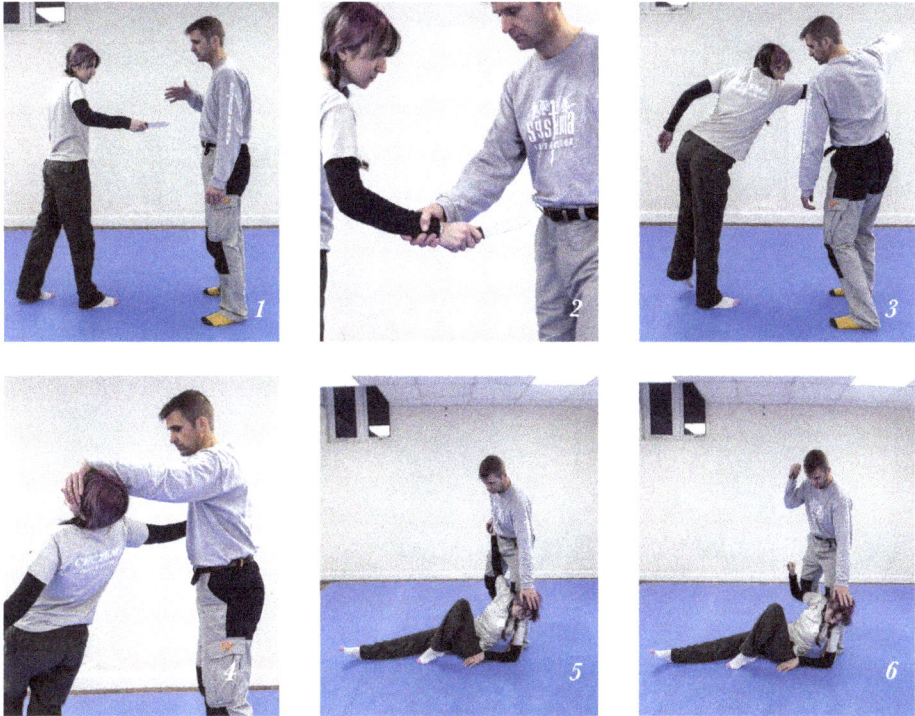

To view the free video of this practise please use the link below:
http://www.matthill.co.uk/combat-videos

"There are several ways to remove stress, the most important are breathing and movement."

\- *Vladimir Vasiliev*

DRILL 21

STAND UP WRESTLING

Stay soft in the body with good structure and keep moving.

The aim of this drill is to teach you to stay soft, supple and to breathe continuously.

The feeder attacks in any way they like with holds and grabs. Start slow and increase the speed and intensity of the grabs as the skill improves.

The receiver's job is to move out of the holds and grabs, not by fighting, but with slippery movements. To the feeder it should feel very fluid. Any tension in the part of the receiver, will give the feeder 'handles' with which to hold the receiver.

Important note: Wrestling or grappling is hard physical work. It is very important to maintain your breathing discipline: in through the nose and out through the mouth. Stay soft in the body with good structure and keep moving constantly.

To view the free video of this practise please use the link below:

http://www.matthill.co.uk/combat-videos

"Begin to feel energised through your practice – be like a dynamo. Breathe, move and relax and you will generate energy as you train"

\- *Matt Hill*

DRILL
22

GO WITH THE FLOW GROUND
A practise in blending

In this drill the feeder comes in to grab or pin the receiver. The job of the receiver is to go with the movement and not resist it. As the receiver yields, they should turn the movement to an advantageous position by twisting, turning or taking the partners balance. An example is shown in the pictures.

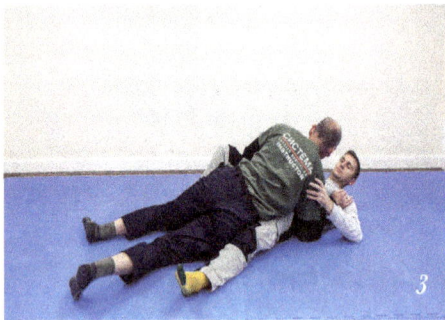

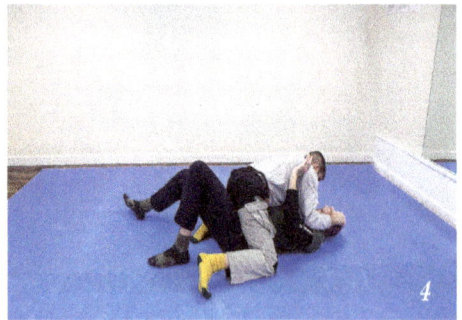

Important point: *Go very slowly at first so that you feel the direction of attack, move smoothly with it and at the same time feel how to turn it to your advantage.*

If you go too fast in the beginning, you will only practise what you know and not learn new skills.

To view the free video of this practise please use the link below:

http://www.matthill.co.uk/combat-videos

DRILL 23

GO WITH THE FLOW STANDING

From reactive to proactive

As per Drill 22, the feeder comes in to grab or pin the receiver. The job of the receiver is to go with the movement and not resist it. As the receiver yields, they should turn the movement to an advantageous position by twisting, turning or taking the partner's balance. An example is shown in the pictures. From standing really focus on incorporating Drill 11: the structure break.

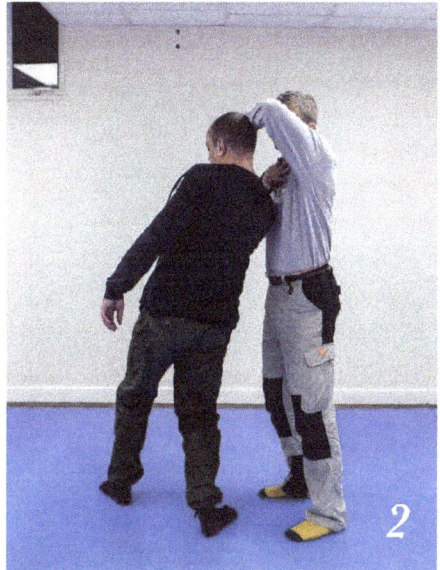

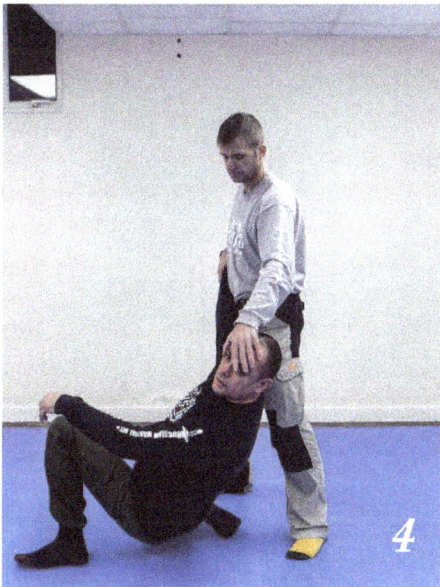

Important point: *Go very slowly at first so that you feel the direction of attack. Move smoothly with it and at the same time feel how to turn it to your advantage. As with all drills, if you go too fast in the beginning, you will only practise what you know and not learn new skills.*

To view the free video of this practise please use the link below:

http://www.matthill.co.uk/combat-videos

DRILL 24

BODY SURFING

Learning to use your body weight to good effect

This is a fun drill to practise, using your weight to good effect in ground movement. The drill starts with the feeder on the ground and the receiver on top. The feeder's job is to roll continually underneath the receiver. The role of the receiver is to 'surf' or ride this movement, maintaining contact and keeping their weight on the feeder. The receiver should be agile and move as needed to maintain contact. Sometimes light and sometimes heavy. Use this drill to develop your mobility, movement, weight transfer and alternating between being light and heavy.

To view the free video of this practise please use the link below:
http://www.matthill.co.uk/combat-videos

"It is when you least want to get up and go training that you are going to get the most out of it personally."

\- *Matt Hill*

DRILL 25

BODY REMOVAL

Teaching efficient body movement

This drill acclimatizes you to pressure and the panic feeling of being crushed. The receiver lies on the floor. The feeder lies across the partner. At this point the receiver should pause, breathe smoothly and make sure that there is no tension or panic in the body. Then feel where the gaps are and find the path of least resistance out from underneath the feeder, without pushing or lifting. This drill teaches good, efficient body movement.

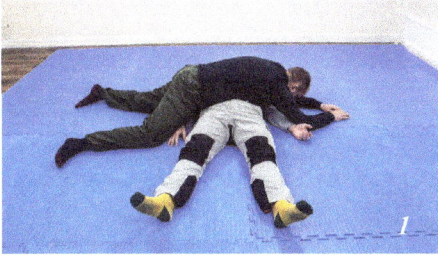

Progression: The feeder should lie across the partner at different angles; on their back, front and side. The receiver should also adopt different positions, front, back and side. When you are comfortable with this then try it with two, three or more people lying across you, stacked on top of each other.

To view the free video of this practise please use the link below:

http://www.matthill.co.uk/combat-videos

"The beauty of Systema is that It provides you with health and skill at the same time.
  - Vladimir Vasiliev"

IN CONCLUSION
Progression on your journey

It is my hope that you will continue your exploration through the concepts outlined in this book over the coming months and years. This book is just a catalyst for further research and practice. As Bruce Lee famously said, 'Use only that which works and take it from any place you can find it.'

The drills outlined in the pages of this book are not meant to be dogmatic. Systema is not a 'frozen' Martial Art. It is continually evolving. With each new person that comes to it, it evolves again. These drills can and should be adapted and mixed with your own experience and knowledge. The permutations are limitless.

If you wish to progress further in your journey you should seek out a good instructor. Vladimir Vasiliev has a useful instructor search tool on his website:

https://www.russianmartialart.com/schoollocator.php

Try not to get frustrated in your progress. I wish you fortune, strength, health and happiness in your journey.

If you have any questions please feel free to contact me through the website www.matthill.co.uk or email wiltshiremartialarts@gmail.com.

Don't forget to get access to your complimentary video of each of the practises outlined in the book by using this link: http://www.matthill.co.uk/combat-videos

Recommended Reading:

Let Every Breath - Vladimir Vasiliev.
Strikes, Soul Meets Body - Vladimir Vasiliev.

Recommended Viewing:

Both Mikhail Ryabko and Vladimir Vasiliev have extensive video collections. Videos for both teachers can be found and purchased from their websites.

Notes

Notes

Notes

Notes

.

—

Lightning Source UK Ltd.
Milton Keynes UK
UKHW051017021118
331642UK00009B/127/P

9 781911 473244